HOW TO USE NETWORKING TO FIND JOB

MANOJ KUMAR SINGH
Entrepreneur, Motivator,
Counselor, Life Enthusiast,
Writer, Soft Skills Trainer

"Happy Networking and Job Searching"

Copyright @2016 Manoj Kumar Singh

All rights reserved.

ISBN-10: 1537511998

ISBN-13:978-1537511993

"Happy Networking and Job Searching"

DEDICATION

I would dedicate this book to all the job seekers and hope that this book gives them decent insight into how to use the networking for complete career growth along with the job finding.

"Happy Networking and Job Searching"

ACKNOWLEDGEMENT

I would like to Thank My Parents, My Gurus, My Friends, My Students, My Colleagues and Even People who never Liked me, because it is they who have taught me how to really attain peace even when things are not in my favor and that there is always a positive side of even a negative.

"Happy Networking and Job Searching"

PREFACE

Human nature is to stay together and to work together. We love to work along people whom we are familiar with. This book contains why and how of using networking to know more people and find job for great career.

"Happy Networking and Job Searching"

"Happy Networking and Job Searching"

CONTENT

Introduction to Networking……………………………...Page No. 7

Types of Networking………………………………........Page No. 8-14

    1. Real World Networking………………………Page No. 8-11

    2. Virtual World Networking……………………Page No.12-14

Advantages of Networking to Find Job……………...Page No. 15-16

Tips of Networking for Job finding…………….........Page No. 17-22

Conclusion…………………………………………………Page No. 23

About the Author………………………………………...Page No. 24

"Happy Networking and Job Searching"

INTRODUCTION TO NETWORKING

We Humans are social animals and we need each others' presence to be able to survive on this planet. We look after each others' back at times of adversity.

Our social nature helps us to interact with each other and most importantly ensures we stick with people whom we like.

Many people will ask what it has to do with the job finding and the professional life.

But the highly successful people will say being social and networking is an important part of professional life, be it for finding a good job or acquiring an important project for the company.

Even as a human nature we love to work with the people whom we know, that makes networking even better tool in job search.

"Happy Networking and Job Searching"

Types of Networking as per the place of Meeting

1. **Real World Networking:**

    This comprise of meeting the person in reality. In the real world you can meet people anywhere while visiting your cousin's birthday party to a grand event where you never wanted to go.

    One should always keep the eye open and mentally prepared when any opportunity comes along but on with some change in the way to convey the message as per the occasion.

"Happy Networking and Job Searching"

Here are some real world places where we meet many people and have chance of networking:

i. **Family and Friends functions-**

Most often family members and friends are the most ignored ones when it comes to finding job. Very few people actually reach out to them for any suggestions.

These functions give you an opportunity to know those family members whom you haven't met for years and don't know what they are doing, you never know how happy some of them may be to help you.

"Happy Networking and Job Searching"

ii. **Meeting Neighbors-**

One may not even think about them but having good neighbors and good relationship with them can also be helpful in search for your job. Either they or anyone they know can become a key to your job search.

iii. **College Alumni meet-**

Some colleges organize annual alumni meet to help their fresher interact with their seniors who are already working.

These events should be taken as a good opportunity to interact with them; you never know who can help you get that break you had been looking for. This even implies for professionals looking for job change.

"Happy Networking and Job Searching"

iv. **Meetings of the Associations or Clubs-**

If you are professional association or any activity club, you get the chance to meet many people there. You must not miss the chance to interact and you never know with whom you share the hobbies or interest; you may end up working with them or for them.

v. **Travelling-**

Life is full of surprises. So expect in yours too. While travelling also there are chances you may meet a person who can help you in your job search. Professionals often exchange their visiting cards while on travel which can be followed up by a good email to initiate talks to the next level.

"Happy Networking and Job Searching"

2. **Virtual World Networking:**

   Enter the digital world and the whole scenario changes. It brings the world at your fingertip and people at the farthest corner of the world face to face with you. Here are some of the Virtual places where we meet and network with other people:

   i. **Chat Groups-**

   There are different apps like WhatsApp, Line, WeChat and Viber etc which have now form important part of our daily life. There are different groups formed which share information and also help to interact with people from different backgrounds.

   Also internet has many options available with site having chat rooms or groups where you can talk and interact with even people from different countries.

"Happy Networking and Job Searching"

ii. **Professional Groups-**

These are special groups formed for the professionals from same background. Here the professionals discuss on the latest trends and also sometimes openings in their company are also shared.

iii. **Social Networking Sites-**

There are various social networking sites which bring people together both at the personal and professional level. Some of leading social site are LinkedIn for professional connections, Facebook for personal and professional, Twitter and Instagram etc.

The choice of social site depends on the work of the professional but everywhere people network with each other, if properly used it forms a powerful tool in job search. Most of the recruiters are also finding talents on these social sites.

"Happy Networking and Job Searching"

iv. **Job Portals/Sites-**

This may not exactly be the direct networking but is a very useful tool for your job search.

Most people will say that job portals are only the place to put your CV but I say Job portals and sites are also great places to actually follow the Hr or the important Leader in the field of your interest.

You can follow them and be updated on latest openings in the companies you are targeting.

Also by accessing the resource sites where some of the top class experts share their views regarding the changing trends in the field will help you to keep updated and be prepared for the interview.

"Happy Networking and Job Searching"

Advantages of Networking to find Job

1. Experienced hiring experts believe success of finding job depends 20% on job applying, 20% on resume and 60% on networking.
2. Networking gives you 10 fold better chance of recruitment.
3. Helps you build references where people will vouch for your skills and potentials etc.
4. You can share your CV with your contacts and get their feedback on it to better prepare for the target industry and position applied for.
5. Many a times some jobs are not even advertised and you may not be aware of the vacancy if not for networking.
6. Networking helps you get preference for at least CV screening or call for the interview over many more who have applied for that single job.

"Happy Networking and Job Searching"

7. Networking helps you connect with unknown people whom you have never met and you get to know them better either face to face or through social media networking. It also improves your peoples' skills.

"Happy Networking and Job Searching"

Tips of Networking for Job Finding

Networking forms an important tool in finding job in present day scenario. As majority of the jobs about 60% are secured through references. These references do not come automatically. The more you socialize and meet more people the better it becomes.

It is difficult to separate out only the contacts from your field but when networking, you may not need that as someone from banking background can know many people from different fields. It is similar in medical profession. Networking when utilized to maximum potential gives an impetuous to your career. However, it's a step by step process and takes time.

"Happy Networking and Job Searching"

One should remember these key points of networking in finding job:

1. **Must have Goals or Strategy-**

    While you go to any event or even when meeting someone online you should prepare your goals that you wish to achieve through this networking opportunity. A better prepared strategy means more success of this networking.

2. **Be Prepared-**

    Most of the people will think it's same as setting goals or strategy. However it's to identify the key people you plan to meet at the networking opportunity and prepare yourself to acquaint to them. When you have done your homework right you have better topics to discuss and make deeper influence.

"Happy Networking and Job Searching"

3. **Show Respect and Build Acquaintance-**

   When you approach the stranger for the networking always remember most of the time the conversation should be about them and not to self obsess. Begin with the gentle topics like sports if man you are talking to. These small conversations will help you build the acquaintance with the stranger, which will then allow you move to other topics.

4. **Seek Information and not Job-**

   Once you have build acquaintance you should not waste the time by talking on something irrelevant. You should mix your questions comprising where the other person works, what's his position and how he/she got the job.

   Company's working environment, how to apply and later you can ask for a review and feedback of you CV. A master networker knows exactly what to say to hint his requirements without revealing neediness.

"Happy Networking and Job Searching"

5. **Listening is a Great tool-**

   Take any soft skill and get a voting done, you will always find Listening to be listed in top 5 if not the number one. Similarly when you are trying to build a network, during the conversation focus more on listening as it gives you more time to think and makes your next move better.

6. **Be positive and happy-**

   People like to talk and interact with positive people. If you are happy with smile on your face you will always make the best impression until you speak something untimed. Remember even the employers want to hire people with positive attitude to work for them.

"Happy Networking and Job Searching"

7. **Apply Filter-**

    It's good to be social and interact with as many people but you should know to filter out the relevant contacts that you should give your maximum time. This way you will get more for your efforts and higher results.

8. **Share Your Experiences-**

    Blogs or speeches at the local groups also help build reputation and forms the part of self branding. On Social Media take part in the group discussions and answer to the queries of others.

9. **Social Media Account-**

    In order to leverage the social media at its fullest, create decent social media accounts and follow the influencers of industry, companies and be part of groups.

"Happy Networking and Job Searching"

10. **Show Gratitude-**

    Never forget to thank the people for their references. If possible follow them up even when you no longer need any help from them. Wish them on important occasions like their birthday, marriage anniversary or even on New Year or any Major Festival.

"Happy Networking and Job Searching"

CONCLUSION

The industries worldwide at present are witnessing a grave shortage of skilled workforce. This shouldn't be misunderstood with the lack of real talent but the problem dwells deep into the system which doesn't train the talents well enough to reach the industry requirements. Networking helps one to get the important feedback to indentify the skills which he needs to work on and get an important reference into the key job requirements.

Networking is an art which is a slow process but once you master it then you can realize its full potential for career growth.